FESTIVALS

IN
REGIONS
AND
SEASONS
OF INDIA

Dr. VIJAYA GUPCHUP

NAVNEET PUBLICATIONS (INDIA) LIMITED

F0531

A Note from the Publishers

In this book, we have presented a series of letters from a grandson to his grandfather, with the grandfather's replies. The subject of the letters is the festivals in India, as they occur within the six Indian seasons.

From this material, it is possible to do so many different activities. For instance, the letters can be treated as a project for dramatic reading, with a child taking the grandson's part while the teacher or parent represents the grandfather. The objective of this project would be to make children aware of the various aspects of Indian tradition and culture while broadening their horizons at the same time.

The letters can be used as stepping stones for correlated activities. Indeed, after reading the letters, the child will enjoy tackling the fun pages with activities, given at the back of the book.

This book has been conceived with the intention of helping children understand and appreciate the multi-faceted culture of the people of India and their own rich heritage.

© **Navneet Publications (India) Ltd. (1999)**

Navneet Publications (India) Ltd.
Bhavani Shankar Road, Dadar, Mumbai - 400 028. INDIA
(Tel. 6662 6565 • Fax : 6662 6470)

Visit us at : www.navneet.com • **e-mail :** publications@navneet.com

Edited by : Chandralekha Maitra

Designed, Illustrated & Processing by : Mind's eye, Mumbai.

Printed at : Printmann, Mumbai - 400 013   1013

INDIA ISBN 978-81-243-0361-0

Price : Rs. 80.00

FESTIVALS IN REGIONS AND SEASONS

FESTIVAL	त्योहार - उत्सव	SOLAR MONTH (English Calender)	LUNAR MONTH (Indian Calender)	SEASON
RATH YATRA	रथयात्रा	JUNE	*JYAISTH* ज्येष्ठ	SUMMER
RAMZAN ID*	रमजान ईद	JULY	*ASHAD* आषाढ	*GREESHMA RITU* ग्रीष्म ऋतु
TEEJ	तीज	JULY	*SHRAVAN* श्रावण	RAINS
NAG PANCHAMI	नागपंचमी	AUGUST		
RAKSHA BANDHAN	रक्षाबंधन			
JANMASHTAMI	जन्माष्टमी			
ONAM	ओणम्			
PATETI	पटेटी			
KHORDAD SAL	खोरदाद साल			
PARYUSHAN	पर्युषण			
GANESH CHATURTHI	गणेश चतुर्थी	SEPTEMBER	*BHADRAPAD* भाद्रपद	*VARSH RITU* वर्षा ऋतु
SAIR-E-GULFAROSHAN	सैर-ए-गुलफरोशन			
DASSERA	दशहरा		*ASHVIN* अश्विन	AUTUMN
DIWALI	दीपावली	OCTOBER		*SHARAD RITU*
GURU PARB	गुरु पर्व	NOVEMBER	*KARTIK* कार्तिक	शरद ऋतु
HANUKAH	हनुकाह		*MARGASHEERSH* मार्गशीर्ष	EARLY WINTER
CHRISTMAS	क्रिसमस (नाताल)	DECEMBER		*HEMANT RITU*
NEW YEAR	नववर्ष	JANUARY	*PAUSH* पौष	हेमंत ऋतु
MAKARA SANKRAT	मकर संक्रांति	JANUARY	*MAGH* माघ	WINTER
PONGAL	पोंगल	FEBRUARY		*SHSHIR RITU*
LOHRI	लोहड़ी			शिशिर ऋतु
SARASWATI POOJA	सरस्वती पूजन	MARCH	*PHALGUN* फाल्गुन	
HOLI	होलीकोत्सव			
GUDI PADVA	गुढी पाढवा	APRIL	*CHAITRA* चैत्र	SPRING
BAISAKHI	बैसाखी	MAY		
EASTER	ईस्टर			
MAHAVIR JAYANTI	महावीर जयंती		*VAISHAKH* वैशाख	*VASANT RITU* वसंत ऋतु
BUDDHA JAYANTI	बुद्ध जयंती			

* Varies every year)

Dear Grandpapa,

Today was my first day of the new term at school. My teacher spoke to us about a project that we would be doing this year. It will be a project on festivals. Our teacher told us to find out something about Indian festivals and then share the information with our classmates.

Grandpapa, you have always told me such lovely stories. Please write and tell me about the festivals of India. I want to make my teacher happy.

Please write to me soon!

Your loving grandson,

Tej

New Delhi

Dear Tej,

I was delighted to receive your letter and hear that you want to know about Indian festivals.

Every region or part of India has its own charm. In north India, it is colder than the flatter plains of south India. But it is not cold all the time. It sometimes becomes warm and at other times even hot. This depends upon the season.

The map of India showing mountains and plains

4

I will tell you about the Indian year and the Indian seasons. But first you must know a bit of interesting historical information.

The British came to India to trade, but eventually ruled our country for nearly 200 years. At this time we adopted their **Gregorian calendar**. This calendar has 12 solar (based on the sun) months in the year, from January to December. As you already know, during these 12 months there are four seasons–spring, summer, autumn and winter.

You might wonder how we have seasons. The earth goes round the sun. The earth's path is called its **orbit**. That part of the earth which faces the sun, has day, while the other part has night. At the same time, the earth spins on its **axis**, which is an imaginary line that runs through the middle or centre of the earth. The two points where the axis passes through the surface of the earth are called the North Pole and the South Pole.

The seasons change because the earth's axis is tilted as the earth moves in its orbit. Let me draw a sketch and show you.

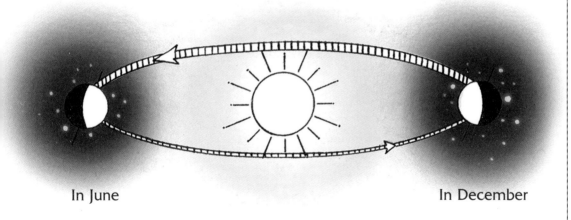

In June   In December

The earth at its June and December positions

You will see that when the pole is tilted towards the sun, we have warmer days. When the pole is tilted away, the days are cold, then it is winter. In this way, seasons are created.

So far we have talked about the Gregorian calendar which is based on the sun. The **Indian calendar** however, is a lunar calendar (it is based on the moon). Indians look at the moon as it becomes full like a ball and then becomes a crescent or a sleeping letter C(∪). When the moon is becoming full it is WAXING. This takes about 15 days. For the next 15 days it

The phases of the moon

is WANING or becoming smaller and smaller, till there is no moon at all in the sky. In other words, 30 days pass between one full moon and the next.

There are 12 months in the Indian calendar also. But unlike the Gregorian calendar which has four seasons, the Indian calendar has six seasons. Most Indian festivals are related to these six Indian seasons. Each season or *ritu* consists of two months. I will give you a table which will make it easy for you to understand.

SEASON		INDIAN MONTHS	GREGORIAN MONTHS
Grishma Ritu	(Summer)	*Jyaishth, Ashadh*	June-July
Varsha Ritu	(Rains)	*Shravan, Bhadrapad*	July-August-September
Sharad Ritu	(Autumn)	*Ashvin, Kartik*	October-November
Hemant Ritu	(Early winter)	*Margashirsh, Paush*	December-January
Shishir Ritu	(Winter)	*Magh, Phalgun*	January-February-March
Vasant Ritu	(Spring)	*Chaitra, Vaishakh*	April-May

You will find that the Indian months and the Gregorian calendar months do not match exactly, sometimes a few days of a particular month fall into the next Indian season.

I hope you have understood about seasons. In my next letter I will tell you about the various festivals related to the different seasons.

Your loving grandpapa

Mumbai

Dear Grandpapa,

Thank you for the information on seasons. My teacher brought a globe and showed us how the earth is tilted on its axis. We saw pictures of the earth moving around the sun. We also learnt how it is summer when the pole is tilted towards the sun. I understand how it is cold when the pole is tilted away from the sun. Our teacher showed us beautiful picture books.

Please tell me about festivals now.

Your loving grandson,

Tej

New Delhi

Dear Tej,

I am going to start with summer festivals. This is for two reasons. A great Indian poet called Kalidasa, who lived 1500 years ago, wrote a poem called *Ritusamhara* (Pageant of Seasons) and divided the year into six seasons, beginning with summer. This is now the traditional Indian way of thinking. The second reason is that you have just finished your summer vacation. My story of festivals will therefore coincide with your school term. So let us begin with summer.

The poet Kalidasa

Grishma Ritu is summer, the hot season. It falls approximately in June and July. Most of the Indian people are farmers and they depend upon nature and the changing seasons to grow their crops. Therefore, in India, seasons have a special meaning and our festival celebrations are linked to the different seasons.

The most important festival in summer is the **Rath Yatra** or the Car Festival. This is celebrated in Puri, Orissa, every year. The story goes that King Indrayumna wanted to build a temple of Vishnu. He asked Vishvakarma, the architect of the gods, to build the temple. Vishvakarma agreed on the condition that no one would be allowed to see him at work. However, the king could not hold back his curiosity and went to see the architect. Vishvakarma became angry and went away without completing his work and thus the images in the temple were left without hands or feet. The king begged to be forgiven, but Vishvakarma would not listen. However, Lord Brahma came to his rescue and breathed life into the limbless images. These are the images that are worshipped even today.

Balaram   *Subhadra*   *Lord Jagannath*

On the day of the *Rath Yatra*, the deity Jagannath, his brother Balaram and sister Subhadra, are placed in huge chariots or *raths*. These *raths* are pulled by hundreds of devotees, from the main temple to another called the Gundicha Mandir. Here they rest for seven days and then return to their own temple.

The year 1996 was a special year for the *Rath Yatra*, for the three idols were newly made. This event is called *nabakalebar* or the symbolic death and rebirth of Lord Jagannath and is held every 12 years. The new idols are made from the wood of selected *neem* trees.

Nowhere in the world do so many people gather to see such a gigantic event. The people also take turns at pulling the *raths*.

> *The English word 'juggernaut', meaning a large heavy truck or an object that crushes whatever is in its path, actually came from the name 'Jagannath' and the event of the huge car procession in Puri.*

The Rath Yatra

Tej, do you know that the *Rath Yatra* gives us a message? It is a message for people belonging to all age groups and all religions and castes. For 'Jagannath' means 'Lord of the Universe' and his message is **"Vasundhaiva Kutumbakam"**, which means 'The world is my family'.

Lord Jagannath's message is for anyone and everyone who will hear it, anywhere in the world.

I hope you have enjoyed the story.

Your loving grandpapa

Mumbai

Dear Grandpapa,

My teacher was very pleased when I told her about Lord Jagannath's message. She said that we must live as one big family. We must forget our differences. What is the meaning of differences?

Our teachers had small *raths* made of wood. In these we placed the statues of Lord Jagannath, his brother Balaram and sister Subhadra. One of my friends called Anagh beat a brass *thali* while another blew the conch. We pulled the *rath* all round the school. We had such fun!

I am learning so much. I want to know more, so please write soon Grandpapa.

Your loving grandson,

Tej

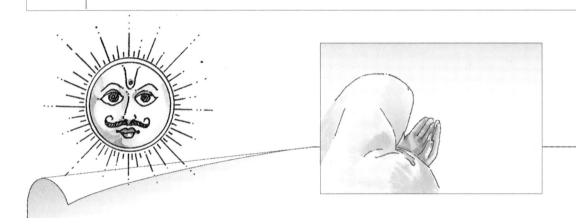

New Delhi

Dear Tej,

I am glad you are beginning to think and to ask questions. When people have 'differences', they do not think alike. Sometimes people quarrel. Many times, people do not agree, but it is not good to quarrel. One of the reasons for having differences is that people believe in different religions.

But you must remember that all religions are good. There is no need to disagree. We must all live as brothers and sisters.

Just as the Hindus, the Christians, the Parsees and the Sikhs have their festivals, so do the Muslims. The Muslims follow the **Arabic lunar calendar**. For them the first night of the new moon brings joy. The sight of the new moon also marks the end of **Ramzan**, which is the month of fasting. The next day is celebrated as **Ramzan Id** or **Id-ul-Fitr**, as the Arabs call it. *Ramzan* is celebrated once a year.

Ramzan is actually the name of a month in the Arabic calendar. It was during this month that Prophet Muhammad was sitting in a cave on a mountain called Mount Hira, when suddenly the Angel Gabriel appeared before him and gave him God's message. This message was later written as the holy book, the *Koran*.

At least once in a lifetime, if health and security of the family permit, Muslims are required to go on pilgrimage to Mecca (in Saudi Arabia) for Haj.
Haj relates to various events in the life of Prophet Abraham. Haj signifies the brotherhood of all Muslims.

Muslims greeting each other on the occasion of Ramzan Id

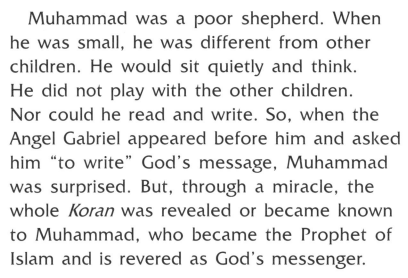

Muhammad was a poor shepherd. When he was small, he was different from other children. He would sit quietly and think. He did not play with the other children. Nor could he read and write. So, when the Angel Gabriel appeared before him and asked him "to write" God's message, Muhammad was surprised. But, through a miracle, the whole *Koran* was revealed or became known to Muhammad, who became the Prophet of Islam and is revered as God's messenger.

During *Ramzan*, Muslims fast. They eat no food and drink no water from sunrise to sunset. They are allowed to have food and water only after sunset. The reason for fasting is to learn discipline and self-control.

After 30 days of fasting, Muslims break their fast with dates or salt. Good food is prepared for *iftar* or the breaking of the fast.

Muslims offering namaz *at a mosque*

Muslims celebrate the end of fasting and call this day *Ramzan Id*. *Id* means a celebration. They make *Sheer Khurma* (vermicelli *kheer*) and *biryani*. New clothes are worn. All the men go to the mosque early in the morning on *Id*, to offer *Id Namaz*, which is a special prayer of thanks.

Relatives visit one another. Elders give the young ones *iddy* or a gift on *Id*. This gift is usually money or sweets. On this day alms are also given to the poor.

Id does not fall in the same month of the Gregorian calendar every year because the Muslim calendar has only 354 days while the Gregorian calendar (from January to December) has 365 days. So the Muslim calendar is 11 days shorter. This is why *Id* can fall in different seasons.

I will talk about the next season and its festivals in my next letter.

Your loving grandpapa

Mumbai

Dear Grandpapa,

Every day we have a period called Conversation.
We tell each other something new that we have learnt.
Of course, I told my class about *Ramzan Id* or *Id-ul-Fitr.*

Iqbal, in my class, was pleased. He told his friend
Saif Khan, who is in a higher class. I now have a new
friend. Saif says it is good to know about each other.
Grandpapa you are right, we should know about other
people. Our teacher tells us that this helps us to forget
our differences.

Please tell me about the next season and its festivals.

Your loving grandson,

Tej

New Delhi

Dear Tej,

I am glad that your teacher is teaching you to be
broad-minded.

The next Indian season is the rainy season or **Varsha Ritu**.
As I said earlier, many people in India earn their living by
farming. So the rains bring happiness. It is time to sow seeds
and see them grow.

In India we get rain from the monsoon winds. These winds bring rain clouds and change the season. The rainy season has many festivals.

You know that your mother is very particular about making certain eats at festival time. Indian women are very devoted to their families. Women also have some special festivals, such as **Teej,** which is celebrated in Rajasthan in the month of *Shravan*.

Women wear brightly coloured clothes. They sing songs about the Goddess Parvati. They make swings by hanging ropes from strong branches of trees. Swinging brings them joy and they feel close to God. Then the women carry the idol of the Goddess Parvati in a procession. They also carry pots (*kalash*) on their heads. The *kalash* is a symbol of the goddess.

Women singing and swinging during Teej *festival*

17

In this season we also celebrate **Nag Panchami** or the festival of snakes. This falls on the fifth day of the waxing moon in the month of *Shravan*. On this day we remember the serpent Ananta. He is Lord Vishnu's serpent

Propitiating snakes on Nag Panchami

and the story goes that after Lord Vishnu created the earth, he rested on the serpent. So, in India, snakes are worshipped and fed milk on this day. People pray to snakes to give them energy and prosperity.

On the full moon day in the month of *Shravan,* we celebrate **Narali Purnima** (Coconut Day) and **Rakshabandhan**. By this time of the year, the fury of the monsoon becomes less and the sea turns calmer. In Maharashtra, fisherfolk offer coconuts, flowers and sweets to the sea god Varun, before they once again go to sea to catch fish.

On *Rakshabandhan* day, sisters tie *rakhis* on their brothers' wrists. Brothers feel proud, because the sisters are asking for their protection.

A Rakhi

Eight days after the full moon in *Shravan* is **Janmashtami,** or the birthday of Lord Krishna. Krishna is believed to have been born at midnight. People offer prayers in temples at night. In some temples a small idol of baby Krishna is put into a cradle at midnight and rocked. In Mathura, where Krishna was born, **Janmashtami** is celebrated with a great deal of fervour and feeling.

Lord Krishna

On the next day, in Mumbai and in other parts of Maharashtra, you know how young boys climb on each others' shoulders and make human pyramids. This is to get to the pot (*matki*) of yoghurt, fruits and money which is tied at a high place. Krishna also loved yoghurt and butter. Quite often, he climbed up high to get the butter pot from the loft.

A human pyramid is formed to reach the pot (matki)

At the end of the monsoon, and also in the month of *Shravan*, is **Onam,** the harvest festival of Kerala. At this time Kerala is lush and green. For four days Kerala comes alive with activity. At Shoranur, Kathakali dancers tell stories from the *Ramayana* and *Mahabharata* through dance movements. At Kottayam, boat races are held. The huge snake-boats have about a hundred oarsmen rowing each boat. As they row, they keep up a joint rhythm by singing songs about well-known people of Kerala.

There are many other festivals in the rainy season. I will write about the rest of them in my next letter.

Your loving grandpapa

The boat race during Onam

A Kathakali dancer

Mumbai

Dear Grandpapa,

   We made *rakhis* with paper and ribbon in school. The girls tied these on our wrists. We promised to protect them. For *Janmasthami,* our teacher brought a small *matki* to school. She tied this earthen pot on a rope. It was not very high. It was fun climbing up on a table and getting to the pot. As a surprise, she had put lots of sweets in it.

   Please write and tell me about the other festivals that fall in the rainy season.

Your loving grandson,

Tej

New Delhi

Dear Tej,

   In one of my earlier letters, I had mentioned different communities. One of these is the Parsi community. The Parsees celebrate **Pateti,** which is the Parsi New Year's eve. On *Pateti* day the Parsees visit the Fire Temple. They promise to live with good thoughts, use good words and perform good deeds.

They offer sandalwood to the Holy Fire.
The men wear their traditional dress called *Dagli* with a Parsi prayer cap.

They stamp *rangoli* patterns with tin moulds to decorate the steps and thresholds of their houses. The front door is decked with flower garlands.
The Parsees visit each

Auspicious objects used by the Parsees

other and spend time feasting. On the next day, they wish each other 'A Happy New Year'.

Six days later, the Parsees celebrate **Khordad Sal**. This is the birthday of their Prophet Zarathustra or Zoroaster. Parsees visit the Fire Temple and Parsi food specialities are made to celebrate the day.

Over 1000 years ago, a group of Zoroastrians or Parsees, left Iran, their homeland and came to India by sea, landing at Sanjan on the western coast. They left Iran because they were not allowed to practise their religion by the Arab rulers. They brought with them the holy fire (Atash Behram) which burns in Udvada even today.

Parsi priests offering prayers

During the last four days of *Shravan* and the first four days of *Bhadrapad*, the Jains celebrate **Paryushan** and learn about the preachings of the 24th *tirthankara*, Mahavir. The Jain religion teaches us how to live a good, pure life and the concept of non-violence. During these eight days of *Paryushan,* the Jains observe various types of fasts.

Lord Mahavir

The Jains believe in speaking the truth (*Satya*); in non-violence (*Ahimsa*); in not stealing and hoarding, and living a pure life (*Brahmacharya*). The Jains also believe it is good to gain knowledge. In fact, the aim of Jain festivals is to get to know oneself and become a better person.

The 14 objects seen in a dream by Mahavir's mother

It is said that Queen Trishala, Mahavir's mother, once dreamt of 14 auspicious objects. In her dream she saw : 1. a lion, 2. an elephant, 3. a bull, 4. goddess Lakshmi, 5. a pair of garlands, 6. the moon, 7. the sun, 8. a flag, 9. a silver *kalasha* or pot, 10. a lake of lotuses, 11. the milky ocean, 12. a divine aerial car, 13. a heap of jewels and 14. a smokeless fire.

The queen narrated her dream to the king and asked him what it meant. The king and other wise men told her that she would give birth to a son who would be a *tirthankara* or an all-knowing person.

Mahavir was born at midnight. It is said that a divine light spread all around. He was named Vardhamana.

During *Paryushan*, the birth and life of Vardhamana Mahavir is read. Throughout his life he always thought of other people and how to help them.

On the ninth day of *Paryushan,* people go to one another and utter the words, *Micchami Dukkadam*, which means 'forgive, forget and be forgiven for any hurt that has been caused during the year'. In this way they spread the message of peace and forgiveness.

On the fourth day of the bright half of *Bhadrapad* is **Ganesh Chaturthi.** Ganesh is the elephant-headed god of wisdom. He is worshipped by the Hindus before starting any good work.

Ganapati procession

25

Ganesh is brought home on Ganesh chaturthi. He is carefully placed on a decorated platform. This is called the *Ganesh Sthapana*. For 10 days there is a great deal of activity. His favourite food — steamed rice-flour *modaks*, stuffed with coconut and *gur*, are made and offered to him. *Aaratis* are sung especially in the evening. After 10 days, Ganesh is immersed in the sea on *Anant Chaturdashi* day.

Before I close, I must tell you about a festival celebrated only in Delhi. It is called **Sair-e-Gulfaroshan, Phool walon-ki-sair** or the Festival of Flowers.

Hindus and Muslims make *pankahs* or fans out of palm leaves.

Delhi

INDIA

A procession of people with flower fans during Sair-e-Gulfaroshan

They are then decorated with flowers. These *pankahs* are taken in a procession. The *Phool walon-ki-sair* starts from the Shamsi Talab near Delhi. They wind their way to the *Dargah* of Qutub Sahib and then go with the fans to the Jagmaya temple at Mehrauli.

What is beautiful about this festival is that both Hindus and Muslims join in the festivities. This should be the mood or spirit of each festival — to get together and forget all differences.

Festivals should be celebrated with joy as they bring people closer. Each festival tells a story with a special message. We must know the story behind each festival and the good thoughts in the story.

These two letters about the rainy season have been rather long as there are many festivals in *Varsha Ritu*.

Your loving grandpapa

Mumbai

Dear Grandpapa,

When I told my teacher about your letter and the Festival of Flowers, I got a golden star for getting the information and telling the class about the spirit of the festival.

We made card-paper fans. We cut out crepe paper flowers and stuck them on the fans. I wish you could see our classroom. It looks so pretty with all the flower fans we have made.

Please tell me more.

Your loving grandson,

Tej

New Delhi

Dear Tej,

I am glad that you are talking about the spirit of the festivals, and that you are learning new things.

The next season is the Indian autumn or **Sharad Ritu** in the months of October and November (the Indian *Ashwin* and *Kartik*). The white jasmine flowers are in bloom. Their sweet smell fills the air. We also see the white bar-headed goose and the white lotus floating on *jheels* and ponds.

Gujarat

W. Bengal

Dandiya Raas

In this season the festivities reach a peak. The nine-day **Navaratri** festival is celebrated mainly in honour of the Goddess Durga. In Gujarat, she is called Goddess Amba. *Navaratri* is celebrated mainly in Gujarat, Karnataka, Tamil Nadu and Bengal.

Mumbai and Gujarat are alive with music and dance in the evenings, and at night young

An image of the Goddess Durga during Durga Puja

girls and boys play the *garba* and the *dandiya raas*, which are dances from Gujarat. Girls wear colourful skirts and blouses called *chaniya-choli* while boys wear *churidar kurtas*.

In Bengal, **Durga Puja** is performed for 9 days. Durga is shown riding a lion and killing the demon Mahishasura (who is evil) with her trident (*trishul*). Thus, we celebrate the triumph of good over evil.

Vijayadashmi or **Dassera** is the tenth day of the bright half of *Ashwin*. There are two stories about *Dassera*. One says that this day celebrates the victory of Durga over the demon Mahishasura.

An effigy of Ravana being burnt

The other story tells us that Rama prayed to Durga for help to defeat the demon king Ravana, who was the king of Lanka. In north India and also in Mumbai and Delhi, giant effigies of Ravana, the ten-headed demon king, are made and burnt on *Dassera* night. This is called *Ramaleela*.

Diwali follows soon after. Diwali is the festival of lights and it brings happiness to all homes. It is believed that on this day Lord Rama returned to Ayodhya after spending 14 years of exile in the forest. Lights are lit to remember the happy event of Rama's homecoming.

Every Hindu house is washed and cleaned for *Diwali*. In Maharashtra, thresholds are decorated with *rangoli*. Tribes called Warlis, who live in the Thane district, near Mumbai, decorate their walls with wonderful designs. So do people in Gujarat and Rajasthan. The goddess Lakshmi is worshipped during *Diwali*. She is the goddess of wealth and prosperity. People perform her *puja* and welcome Lakshmi into their homes, hoping that it will bring them happiness and prosperity.

Diwali is also the time when sweetmeats and gifts are exchanged.

A lighted lamp is considered an auspicious or holy symbol all over the world. Jews, Roman Catholics, Christians, Hindus, Buddhists and Jains all light lamps. Parsees light an oil lamp (diya), before visiting a fire-temple. Lamps are considered by all these communities as symbols of purity.

Lamps (diyas) *lit during Diwali*

People wear new clothes and buy jewellery. There is a great deal of excitement at *Diwali* time. *Diwali* is the last day of the Gujarati year. Most Hindus celebrate the day after *Diwali* as the New Year. The word *Diwali* brings before you a picture of flickering oil lamps. The oil in the lamps is like knowledge. The more you learn, the brighter your mind becomes. In my next letter, I will talk about a festival of the Sikhs.

Your loving grandpapa

A Warli *painting*

Mumbai

Dear Grandpapa,

In school we drew pictures of Ravana. One of the classes enacted the festival of *Dassera* for their assembly. The demon Mahishasura was very fierce and he put up a long fight for 9 days before he was killed.

For *Diwali* a potter came to our school and showed us how to make *diyas* on the potter's wheel. We then painted the *diyas* and took them home.

I am waiting eagerly to hear about the Sikhs in your next letter.

Your loving grandson,

Tej

New Delhi

Dear Tej,

I see that you are learning many interesting things in school to do with festivals.

Guru Parb is celebrated on the full moon night in the month of *Kartik*. This festival, therefore, falls in *Sharad Ritu* or autumn. *Guru Parb* marks the birth of Guru Nanak, who founded the Sikh religion. He believed that all people are equal and that the path to right living is by serving and helping other human beings.

Two days before his birthday, the holy book of the Sikhs, the *Guru Granth Sahib*, is taken up for reading. The reading is carried on day and night without interruption. On *Guru Parb* day, the *Guru Granth Sahib* is taken out in processions from the four famous *Gurudwaras* or Sikh temples of Amritsar (in Punjab), Patna (in Bihar); Anandpur (in Punjab) and Nanded (in Maharashtra).

The Guru Granth Sahib *being read*

The Golden Temple at Amritsar

Guru Govind Singh, the last Guru of the Sikhs, ordered that his disciples must take Pahul *(baptism or vow) and wear the five K's :* Kesh *(long hair),* Kara *(iron bangle),* Kank *(comb worn in the hair),* Katch *(short trousers) and the* Kirpan *(sword). The Kesh represents a vow, the* Kank *is worn to keep the hair clean. The* Kara *stands for the determination to give up all luxury, the* Katch *must always be worn to be ever ready and the* Kirpan *proclaims that the Sikhs are a martial race.*

On this day *langars* or community kitchens, are organized.

All the people who visit the *Gurudwaras* sit together and share a tasty meal. *Prasad* is served.

In my next letter I will write to you about *Hemant Ritu*.

Your loving grandpapa

A langar *meal*

Mumbai

Dear Grandpapa,

Even my teacher looks forward to your letters to me. I share what you tell me with my class. My teacher also loves to listen to me. A girl called Tripti wrote a story about the Sikhs. She has been to many *langars*. Our teacher read out her story to us. Can you tell me something about other communities that live in India and their festivals?

Your loving grandson,

Tej

New Delhi

Dear Tej,

Here is something that you have asked for. The next season is early winter or **Hemant Ritu**. The Gregorian months of December and January coincide with *Margashirsh* and *Paush* in India.

We are now going to talk about the Jews who live in India. The Jews pray at the synagogue, just as the Hindus pray in a temple and Muslims pray in a mosque.

The Jewish festival of **Hanukah,** which means 'dedication', lasts for 8 days. This is the story of *Hanukah*. At the temple of Jerusalem, eternal lamps, which symbolised the presence of God, were always kept burning. But the Greeks invaded Jerusalem and put out the lamps. Eventually, the Jews recaptured Jerusalem and the temple was dedicated to God again by lighting the lamps. A miracle took place then, and the festival of *Hanukah* commemorates what happened.

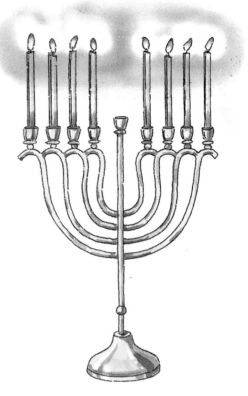

The nine-branched Jewish menorah

When the moment came to relight the candles, there was only enough oil to keep them burning for one day. However, special prayers were offered and somehow the lamps kept burning for eight days, until more oil arrived!

Families and friends gather together and light the special nine-branched candlestick called *menorah* or *Hanukiah*.

On the first evening one candle is lit. The next day, the second candle is lit and so on, until on the eighth evening, all eight candles are burning. The ninth candle is called the *shammas* or the 'servant' candle. It is used to light all the other candles.

Potato *Latkes* or pancakes, are cooked in oil and eaten as a reminder of the miracle. Cards and gifts are exchanged and the game of *dreidels* is played, though not in India.

The *dreidels* have four sides and are spun like tops. Each side has a Hebrew letter written on it which begins the words "A Great Miracle Happened There".

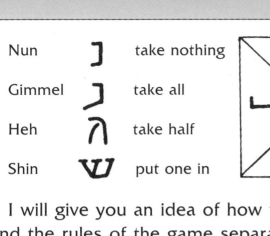

Nun	]	take nothing
Gimmel	]	take all
Heh	ת	take half
Shin	ש	put one in

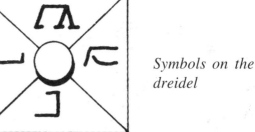

Symbols on the dreidel

I will give you an idea of how to make a card-paper *dreidel* and the rules of the game separately. Now we will go on to the next festival which is **Christmas**.

The Christians celebrate *Christmas* on the 25th of December. It is the birthday of Jesus Christ. Not only in India, but all over the world, people rejoice on this day.

Long, long ago, there lived a Roman Emperor called Caesar Augustus. One day, the Emperor announced that all the Jews in the empire would be counted.

In the town of Nazareth, lived a humble Jewish couple named Joseph and Mary. Every Jew was asked to present himself in his hometown by December 25th.

Joseph, Mary and the baby Jesus

Santa Claus driving his sleigh pulled by reindeer

So, Joseph and Mary left for Bethlehem, in order to register their names. After the long journey, they reached Bethlehem late in the evening. The town was crowded with visitors who had also come to register their names. All the inns were full. Mary and Joseph had to take shelter in a stable. That night, Mary gave birth to a baby. She wrapped him up in swaddling clothes (narrow strips of cloth) and laid him in a manger. Some shepherds were watching over their flock of sheep nearby. Suddenly, an angel appeared before them and announced the birth of Jesus. The shepherds were naturally curious to see the baby and were guided to the stable by a beautiful star. The shepherds saw the baby Jesus and offered their prayers.

Jesus was the Son of God, who came to earth to guide men and show them how to live a life of Truth.

On *Christmas* eve, church bells ring and *Christmas* carols are sung. The *Christmas* tree is decorated in homes. Presents are exchanged. Santa Claus is believed to visit homes and leave presents for good children. *Christmas* is a happy day for all.

A week after *Christmas* comes the **New Year**. This falls on January 1st. It is the first day of the first month of the Gregorian calendar. It is celebrated all over the world. New Year resolutions are made by both young and old people. It is good to keep these.

Your loving grandpapa

The most popular of all Christmas carols is perhaps Silent Night, Holy Night. Joseph Mohr, pastor of a little church in Oberndorf, Austria, wrote the words on Christmas eve, 1818, and Franz Gruber, the church organ player, composed the music the same evening and played it at the midnight mass.

A decorated Christmas tree with presents piled under it

Mumbai

Dear Grandpapa,

We made card-paper *dreidels* and played the game in school. I got quite a few sweets. Then we sang *Christmas* carols. We also made *Christmas* trees, angels and stockings for craft. I hung up my stocking and do you know what I got? I got a present! Mummy says that Santa is pleased with me.

Please tell me more about another season.

Your loving grandson,

Tej

New Delhi

Dear Tej,

Your *Christmas* holidays must have started and it should be pleasant in Mumbai now.

Here in north India, it is cold. Yes, the next Indian season is **Shishir Ritu** or winter,

Children flying kites on Makara Sankranti *day*

which begins around January and lasts till March. It corresponds to the Indian months of *Magh* and *Phalgun*.

The important festival of **Makara Sankranti** falls in January, that is in the month of *Magh*. Here I have to explain why *Makara Sankranti* falls on 14th January every year, while the other festivals have dates that vary.

As you know, the earth moves around the sun in an orbit. It takes the earth one year to go round the sun. During this movement, the earth's axis is tilted. On 22nd December, the South Pole is closest to the sun. Six months later, in June, it is the North pole's turn to be close to the sun. To the people on earth, it seems that the sun starts moving from the south to the north in December. This movement in the northerly direction is called *Uttarayana*. It is believed that *Uttarayana* begins on *Makara Sankrati,* that is 14th January, and it is a fixed day in the Gregorian calendar.

In Maharashtra, sweets made of *til* (sesame) are exchanged with the words '*Til gul ghya ani god, god bola*', which means 'eat the sweet and speak sweetly'. It is also a day for flying kites. In Gujarat, there are international kite-flying competitions and thousands of colourful kites fill the sky!

In other parts of India, like Tamil Nadu and Andhra Pradesh in the south, it is the end of the harvest season and **Pongal** is celebrated.

The first day of *Pongal* is celebrated with the family. *Kolam* designs are made with rice flour outside the house. Doorways are decorated with mango leaves and plaited coconut leaves.

On the next day, people offer thanks to the sun because the

A kolam *design*

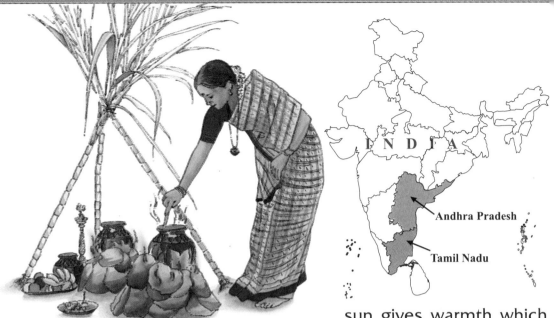

A woman cooking the rice and milk dish during Pongal

sun gives warmth which helps the crops grow well. Huge stalks of sugar cane decorate the courtyard. These are held over the pot in which sweet rice cooked in milk is prepared. Everybody asks "Has the milk boiled?" This boiling over of the *Pongal* dish stands for plenty, meaning that the harvest has been good.

The third and last day of *Pongal* is dedicated to the cattle who have helped to reap the harvest.

In north India, *Lohri* is celebrated at this time. Sugarcane juice, jaggery and sesame (*til*) sweets are distributed. Huge bonfires are lit, and sweets and rice are offered to the fire.

After this comes **Vasant Panchami** or **Saraswati Puja**. Saraswati is the goddess of learning and knowledge.

A bonfire during lohri

In Bengal, Saraswati is regarded as the daughter of Shiva and Durga. Her sister is Goddess Lakshmi and her brothers are Ganesh and Kartik. For *Saraswati Puja*, books are placed in front of Saraswati, along with earthen inkpots and bamboo quills. The ink is made from unboiled milk, water, a pinch of red-coloured powder and silver glitter called *avro*.

An image of Goddess Saraswati

The next day, before the goddess is immersed, the *Saraswati mantra* is written on *bel* leaves, using the milk-ink and quills to write. All children dip their bamboo quills into the earthen inkpots and write *Aum nama Saraswatyai namah*. The goddess is then immersed and the books are put back in their places.

Playing with colour during Holi

Now the biting cold of winter has passed and **Holi** comes in the month of *Phalgun*.

Holi is celebrated with great gaiety. Coloured water is squirted on friends and passers-by. People are joyful because *Holi* celebrates the victory of good over evil, like the stories of Durga and Rama during *Dassera* and *Diwali*.

The story of *Holi* goes like this. King Hiranyakashyapu had become very proud and powerful and wanted to be worshipped as a god. His own son Prahlad refused, as he was

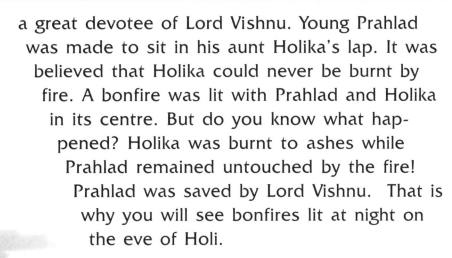

a great devotee of Lord Vishnu. Young Prahlad was made to sit in his aunt Holika's lap. It was believed that Holika could never be burnt by fire. A bonfire was lit with Prahlad and Holika in its centre. But do you know what happened? Holika was burnt to ashes while Prahlad remained untouched by the fire! Prahlad was saved by Lord Vishnu. That is why you will see bonfires lit at night on the eve of Holi.

We have now come to the end of the fifth Indian season. Only one more season with its own festivals remains.

Your loving grandpapa

Mumbai

Dear Grandpapa,

I am feeling excited but sad at the same time that our letters about seasons and festivals are coming to an end. For *Holi* we cut out *pichkaris* of paper. They look like the doctor's injection syringes. We also drew our own pictures and blew colour on them through straws. It was colourful and we had such fun! I have learnt so much! I am eagerly waiting to hear from you.

Your loving grandson,

Tej

Dear Tej,

Although our letters about seasons and festivals are coming to an end, the seasons and festivals themselves form a continuous cycle in our lives. They go on... and on... and on... Now the last season is **Vasant Ritu** or spring. The Gregorian months of March, April and May make up the Indian months of *Chaitra* and *Vaishakh* which form this season.

The gudi

Gudi Padva, is the Maharashtrian New Year. It is also called *Ugadi* in parts of Andhra Pradesh and Karnataka. It falls on the first day of the month of *Chaitra*. People hoist a pole with a shining silver or brass metal vessel fastened to a flowing silk cloth called *gudi*. Garlands of sweet, sugary *battasa*, neem leaves and flowers are tied to the banner. The story goes that Lord Brahma created the whole universe on this day. The *gudi* is tied outside the house, a new *Panchang* (almanac) is placed before the *gudi* and a *puja* with *haldi* (turmeric), *kumkum* (red powder), *chandan* (sandalwood paste) and rice is performed. The custom is to eat a couple of bitter *neem* leaves fried in ghee and mixed with sugar. *Neem* leaves are antiseptic and they are eaten on *Gudi Padva* to ensure good health.

The 13th day of the bright half of *Chaitra*, is the birthday of Mahavir, the 24th *Tirthankara* of the Jains. Remember, we have talked about his message during *Paryushan*.
On **Mahavir Jayanti**, Jains visit their temples (*Derasars*) and eat wholesome food. They listen to stories of the right way to live and they also give money to save cows from slaughter as a form of *ahimsa* (non-violence).

Sravanbelgola (Karnataka) attracts thousands of Jain pilgrims during the *Mahamastak abhishek* the head-anointing ceremony of Lord Bahubali, popularly known as Gomateshwara, which takes place once every twelve years.

The seventeen-metre - high statue of Gomateshwara

Baisakhi marks the first day of the month of *Vaishakh*. In fact, it is the beginning of the Hindu year in north India. It is time to reap the harvest. Everyone is thankful for a good harvest. In Punjab, they do the *Bhangra* dance to celebrate the Baisakhi festival.

Punjab

INDIA

Bhangara dancers

On this day, Guru Gobind Singh founded the *Khalsa* and gave Sikhism its modern form.

Christians celebrate **Easter**. *Easter Sunday* falls some time between March 21 and April 25.

There is a period of 40 days before *Easter* called *Lent*. *Lent* is a time of prayer and fasting to remember Jesus Christ's 40-day fast in the desert. During the week before *Easter Sunday*, church services remind us of the last days of Christ's life on earth. *Good Friday* marks the day when Christ was crucified and died. It is called *Good Friday* because Christians believe that Jesus Christ laid down his life for the good of us all. But *Easter Sunday* is a day of great rejoicing because Jesus rose from the dead on this day! It is, therefore, a time of new life for everyone.

Easter eggs in a basket

Easter is a spring festival and there are many symbols which are associated with it. One of the best-known *Easter* symbols is the Easter egg. The Easter egg is a symbol of life because in all living creatures life begins in the egg. The chick also stands for new life. The sun symbolizes good fortune, the rooster, fulfilment of wishes, the deer, good health and flowers stand for love. I am sure you make many colourful things for *Easter*.

On the full moon day of *Vaishakh* is **Buddha Jayanti**, when Gautam Buddha was born to Queen Mahamaya and King Suddhdhana, in the Lumbini grove in Nepal.

The Buddha's teachings have spread far and wide. It is said that he sat under a *Bodhi* or *Peepal* tree to gain knowledge. The Buddha taught that people can find peace and contentment in life by getting rid of selfish wishes. This can be done by thinking of and caring for others just as we do for ourselves. People should not steal, cheat or become angry, he said. Also, we should never kill or harm any living being.

Spring is the time when nature gives us many gifts. It is the season that gives life to everything. Festivals help us remember the goodness of nature. They bring people together in friendship, love and joy. They teach us the message of unity and harmony and peace. This is why festivals are such an important part of our lives.

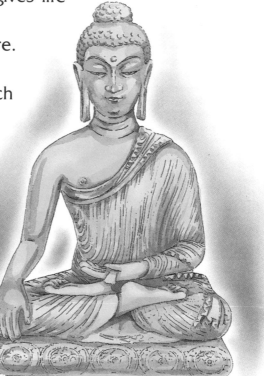

Lord Buddha

I hope you have learnt something useful and will pass on the message of love, harmony and peace to your friends.

Your loving grandpapa

GLOSSARY

adopted	:	took as their own
aarati	:	a form of Prayer
aerial	:	belonging to the air
almanac	:	a book containing information about auspicious hours and days of the year
antiseptic	:	something which prevents infection in a wound
to associate	:	to join with
aum namah		
Saraswatyai namah	:	O, Goddess Saraswati, I bow to you (A prayer written at the time of *Saraswati pooja*)
axis	:	a line, real or imaginary, on which something revolves
to coincide	:	to occur at the same time
communities	:	groups of people having common beliefs and customs
concept	:	an idea
contentment	:	satisfaction
continuous	:	without a break
corresponds	:	is the same as
crescent	:	the thin half circle formed by the moon as it wanes
crucified	:	nailed by the hands and feet to a cross of wood
curiosity	:	eagerness to know
decked	:	dressed up
dedicated	:	devoted to somebody or something
deity	:	a god or goddess
devoted	:	to be very loyal and loving towards someone
devotees	:	people who believe in a religion and follow a saint or a seer
divine	:	belonging to God
exile	:	being sent away from one's own country or native land to live in forests
fervour	:	a warm feeling or enthusiasm
fulfilment	:	completion
fury	:	anger; force
gigantic	:	very big; huge; enormous
harmony	:	living together happily
historical	:	an event of the past
hoarding	:	storing, collecting to create a scarcity
hoist	:	to fly a flag on a pole
illiterate	:	a person who cannot read or write
immerse	:	to put something in water and let it sink
international	:	of different countries or nations

jaggery	:	*gur*
jheel	:	lake
langar	:	a community meal eaten in a Sikh Gurudwara
limbless	:	without arms or legs; handicapped
loft	:	a room or space immediately under the roof
manger	:	a wooden box in which food is put for horses and cattle
mantra	:	holy words
miracle	:	an unbelievable and strange happening
modern	:	recent, of the present time
mould	:	a hollow dish of a certain shape which can be used to make sweets
to narrate	:	to tell or report
non-violence	:	lack of violence or force
orbit	:	the path on which the earth moves around the sun
to organise	:	to arrange methodically
performing	:	doing
plaited	:	interwoven; braided (like hair is)
prosperity	:	good fortune; wealth
quill	:	a bamboo or reed pen
recaptured	:	took again
register	:	a written record which is regularly kept
resolutions	:	firm decisions taken at the beginning of the new year
revealed	:	made known; disclosed
revered	:	respected
serpent	:	a snake
serving	:	a portion of something
to slaughter	:	to kill an animal for food
specialities	:	special food made only on festivals
to squirt	:	to force water out of a narrow opening
stalks	:	stems of plants
swaddling clothes	:	narrow strips of cloth used to wrap around a newborn baby
symbolic	:	a picture or custom representing a belief
synagogue	:	a Jewish place of worship
threshold	:	the entrance of a house
tradition	:	a belief or custom that is passed on from parents to children
to wane	:	to become smaller slowly
to wax	:	to become larger slowly
wealth	:	riches

AUTHOR'S NOTE TO TEACHERS AND PARENTS

The activity pages are based on the five senses which come into play very sharply during festival time.

The first worksheet is connected with the sense of **sight**. The clues are given at the bottom of the page and the child searches for the required words in the Diwali lamp. The worksheet falls within the Wordsearch category.

The second worksheet is based on the sense of **touch**. The child counts the number of petals of each flower and matches the number of letters in the words given below. In other words, each flower has a different number of petals to match the number of letters in each word.

The third worksheet sharpens the child's sense of **hearing** and increases his or her power of English expression. The number of empty dashes corresponds to the number of letters in the word.

The fourth worksheet uses the sense of **smell** with reference to festival time. Here again, the child matches the number of empty spaces to the number of letters in the given word or words.

The fifth worksheet can be tackled after the child is familiar with all the letters of the grandson and grandfather. The worksheet sums up the different foods we **taste** during the festivals talked about in this book.

As an additional activity, there is a page with instructions on how to make and play a dreidel game as it is done during the Jewish festival of Hanukah. The game, as the grandfather says, is truly enjoyable and enhances the child's mathematical skills at the same time.

The letters also suggest art and craft possibilities, such as the making of floral fans, cards and a host of other activities.

It is hoped that these series of letters will inculcate a spirit of eagerness to learn and do more and thereby make the teaching-learning process a success.

WORDSEARCH
On festive days, we see ...

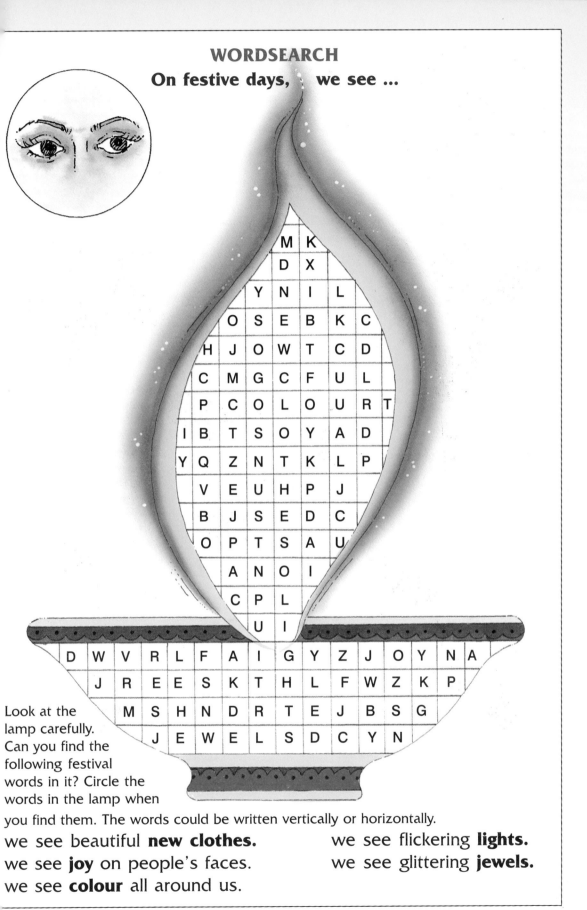

Look at the lamp carefully. Can you find the following festival words in it? Circle the words in the lamp when you find them. The words could be written vertically or horizontally.

we see beautiful **new clothes.**

we see **joy** on people's faces.

we see **colour** all around us.

we see flickering **lights.**

we see glittering **jewels.**

FEEL-WORDS
On festive days, we touch...

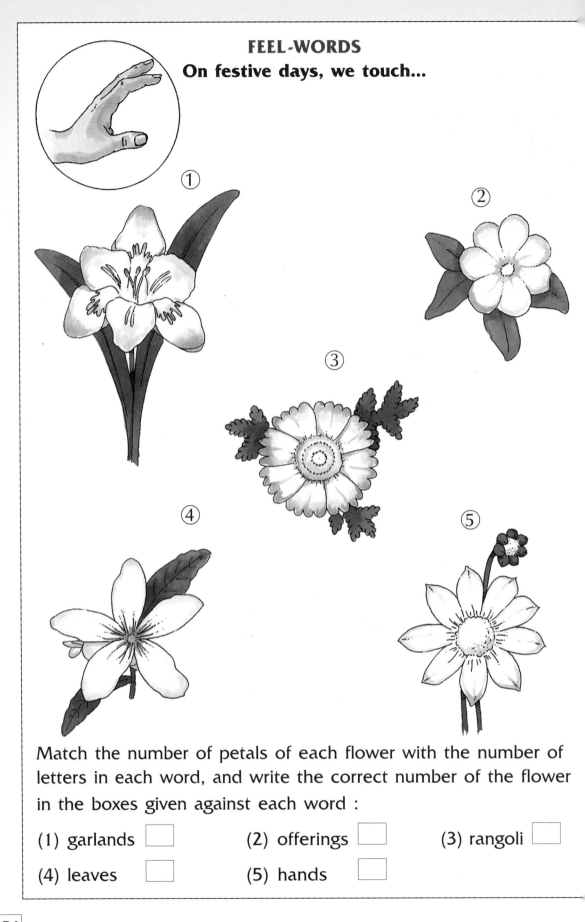

Match the number of petals of each flower with the number of letters in each word, and write the correct number of the flower in the boxes given against each word :

(1) garlands ☐   (2) offerings ☐   (3) rangoli ☐

(4) leaves ☐   (5) hands ☐

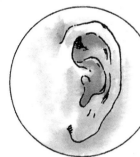

WORDSOUNDS

On festive days, we hear ...

Find the correct sounds and write them in the blanks.

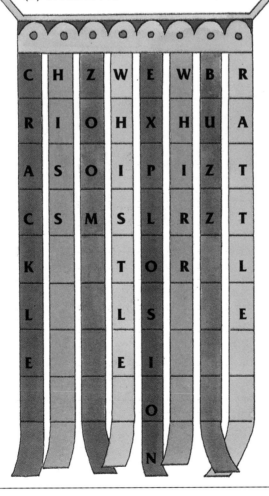

(1) We hear the _ _ _ _ of the snakes.

(2) We hear the _ _ _ _ of the rockets.

(3) We hear the _ _ _ _ _ _ of the catherine wheel.

(4) We hear the _ _ _ _ _ _ _ _ of sparklers.

(5) We hear the _ _ _ _ _ _ _ _ _ _ of bombs.

(6) We hear the _ _ _ _ _ _ _ of small crackers.

(7) We hear the _ _ _ _ _ _ _ _ of a parachute.

(8) We hear the _ _ _ _ of children.

SMELL-WORDS
On festive days, we smell ...

_ _ _ _ _
_ _ _ _ _ _ _ _

_ _ _ _ _ _ _

_ _ _
_ _ _ _ _

_ _ _ _ _ _ _

Match the number of dashes with number of letters of the words below and write them in the correct places :

(1) oil lamps

(2) agarbatti (incense stick)

(3) flowers

(4) burnt crackers

(5) chandan‾ (sandalwood)

TASTE-WORDS
On festive days, we taste ...

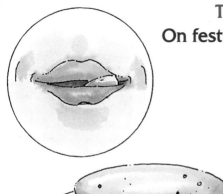

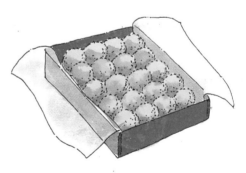

Write the correct word in the place given below the picture.

(1) laddoos   (2) panchamrut   (3) latke jewish pancake

(4) sheer khurma   (5) fruit cake   (6) halwa

LETTER WRITING

Letters help us to communicate or keep in touch with people anywhere in the world. A letter can take your thoughts across thousands of kilometres to visit a friend or your family. It can say thank you, give information, send an invitation or even help a person apply for a job.

It is good to know the proper way to write each kind of letter.

Now let us discuss the five parts of a friendly letter :

(a) The heading

The heading has two parts.

(1) The writer's address with City and Pin Code number and

(2) the date on which the letter is being written.

Here is an example:

40, Tagore Street,

Santacruz (West), Mumbai 400 054.

15th June, 1999

(b) The greeting

The greeting tells you to whom the letter is written. It begins at the left-hand margin and is followed by a comma. For example, a letter may begin with 'Dear Grandpapa', like those given in this book.

(c) The body

The body of the letter gives the news. It has a different paragraph for each topic you want to write about.

Always read over your letters to check for mistakes. Try to write as neatly as possible.

(d) The closing

This is a way of saying good-bye. "Lovingly", "With Love", "Your friend", "Your loving", are correct ways of closing letters to people dear to you.

Please note that the closing words are written on the bottom right-hand side of your letter.

(e) The signature

The signature is your name. Even in a type-written letter, the signature should be handwritten. This goes with the closing words:

With love,
Rahul

Planning a letter

Planning a letter helps you to remember what you want to write.

(1) Choose just a few topics and start with the one which would most interest the person to whom you are writing.

(2) Before you start, be sure to read over the last letter you have received from the person to whom you are writing and answer any questions he/she may have asked.

(3) A friendly letter must sound like a lively conversation. A good letter-writer makes the reader feel he can see, hear, smell and feel what the writer did! If you learn to write such letters, your friends will be eager to receive them. Make letter writing a habit, it is a pleasure to write and receive letters.

Addressing the envelope

Fold your letter and put it into an envelope.

Write the name and address of the person to whom you are sending the letter in the centre of the envelope, like this :

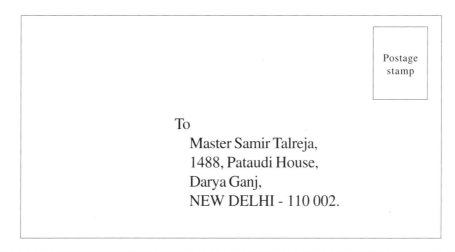

DREIDEL GAME

The Dreidel Game is an important part of the jewish festival of Hanukah. The Dreidel game is an excellent game for practice in Maths. Ask your teacher to play the game in class. This is how you play it :

(1) Each player puts a set amount of sweets or nuts or any other items into the centre of the table.

(2) Then each one takes a turn to spin the dreidel.

(3) Sweets are won or lost depending upon how the spinner lands.

(4) Nun means take nothing, therefore nothing will happen, so go on to the next person.

(5) Heh means take half, so the player will get half of the sweets from the centre pile.

(6) Shin means put one in when the spinner lands on shin, one item is added to the centre pile.

(7) Gimmel means take all. This allows everything to be taken from the centre pile.

(8) When each player has had a turn, the first round is over. Each player then counts the number of sweets that he has collected. The player who has the largest number of sweets is the winner.

The spinner can be made from card paper and the Hebrew symbols can be drawn on it. Use the template of the dreidel given on the next page and follow the instructions of how to make the dreidel. Then pierce a pencil through the spinner and start the game.

Instructions To Make The Dreidel:

The spinner or dreidel can be made with card paper and a pencil which is pushed through the centre of the spinner. Hebrew symbols are printed on the faces of the spinner.

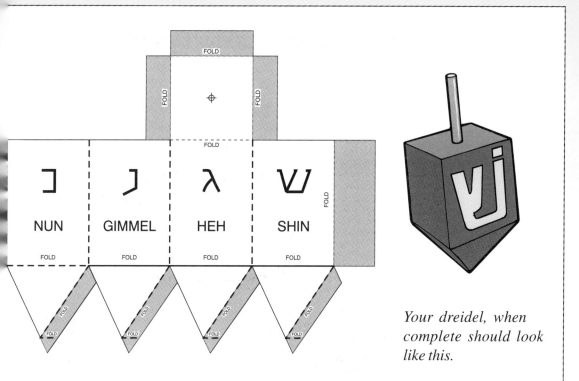

NUN | GIMMEL | HEH | SHIN

Your dreidel, when complete should look like this.

Here are the instructions :

(1) Take a card paper of A4 size i.e.   29 cms x 21.5 cms

(2) Trace the figure on the card paper. Be careful to draw solid lines and dotted lines as shown. Solid lines are meant for cutting; dotted lines are for folding.

(3) Cut along the solid lines (avoid cutting on the dotted lines).

(4) Fold along the dotted lines.

(5) Now form a 'SOLID' by folding the card paper along the 'FOLD' lines.

(6) Areas shaded are to be glued by tucking them in to complete the 'SOLID' having a rectangular box shape at the top with a hopper at the bottom.

(7) Pierce a small hole with a pointed pin on the point marked 'O' on the top of the solid.

(8) Slide a pencil through so that the pencil point emerges out of the pointed hopper bottom.

(9) Your dreidel is now ready for spinning on the pencil point.

HOW TO MAKE POTATO LATKES

Mrs. Sopher from Israel, has sent this recipe for Potato Latkes eaten during Hanukah.

What you need :

(1) 1600 g potatoes

(2) 2 large onions

(3) 50 g self-raising flour

(4) Oil

How to proceed :

Peel and grate the potatoes and drain. Grate the onions and mix the potatoes and flour. Shape into small, flat pancakes and shallow fry on both sides in hot oil until golden brown.

Perhaps you can help your mummy make them.

HOW TO MAKE AN ENVELOPE

When completed, the envelope will ←look like this :

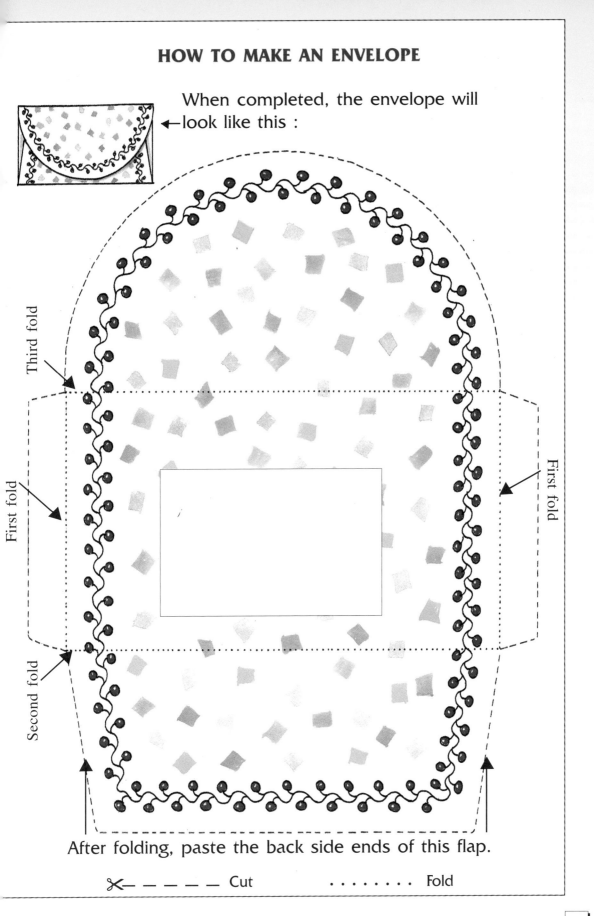

Third fold

First fold

First fold

Second fold

After folding, paste the back side ends of this flap.

✂ — — — — — Cut   . . . . Fold